Celebrating the birthday of

_____

Name

Thoughts

The best picture:

Name

Thoughts

The best picture:

Name

Thoughts

The best picture:

Name

Thoughts

The best picture:

Name

Thoughts

The best picture:

Name

Thoughts

The best picture:

Name

Thoughts

The best picture:

Name

Thoughts

The best picture:

Name

Thoughts

The best picture:

Name

Thoughts

The best picture:

Name

Thoughts

The best picture:

Name

Thoughts

The best picture:

Name

Thoughts

The best picture:

Name

Thoughts

The best picture:

Name

Thoughts

The best picture:

Name

Thoughts

The best picture:

Name

Thoughts

The best picture:

Name

Thoughts

The best picture:

Name

Thoughts

The best picture:

Name

Thoughts

The best picture:

Name

Thoughts

The best picture:

Name

Thoughts

The best picture:

Name

Thoughts

The best picture:

Name

Thoughts

The best picture:

Name

Thoughts

The best picture:

Name

Thoughts

The best picture:

Name

Thoughts

The best picture:

Name

Thoughts

The best picture:

Name

Thoughts

The best picture:

Name

Thoughts

The best picture:

Name

Thoughts

The best picture:

Name

Thoughts

The best picture:

Name

Thoughts

The best picture:

Name

Thoughts

The best picture:

Name

Thoughts

The best picture:

Name

Thoughts

The best picture:

Name

Thoughts

The best picture:

Name

Thoughts

The best picture:

Name

Thoughts

The best picture:

Name

Thoughts

The best picture:

Name

Thoughts

The best picture:

Name

Thoughts

The best picture:

Name

Thoughts

The best picture:

Name

Thoughts

The best picture:

Name

Thoughts

The best picture:

Name

Thoughts

The best picture:

Name

Thoughts

The best picture:

Name

Thoughts

The best picture:

Name

Thoughts

The best picture:

Name

Thoughts

The best picture:

Name

Thoughts

The best picture:

Name

Thoughts

The best picture:

Name

Thoughts

The best picture:

Name

Thoughts

The best picture:

Name

Thoughts

The best picture:

Name

Thoughts

The best picture:

Name

Thoughts

The best picture:

Name

Thoughts

The best picture:

Name

Thoughts

The best picture:

Name

Thoughts

The best picture:

Impressum
Angaben gemäß § 5 TMG
Stefan Fanslau
Erlenweg, 4
61352 Bad Homburg
Germany

Contact:
E-Mail: stefan.fanslau@gmx.de

Made in United States
Orlando, FL
18 September 2023

37040707R00067